Exploring Bowland and the Hodder

with

Ron Freethy

Contents

Published by Countryside Publications Limited, School Lane, Brinscall, Chorley, Lancashire.
Text © R. Freethy, 1987
Printed by Tamley-Reed Limited.
ISBN 0 86157 264 5

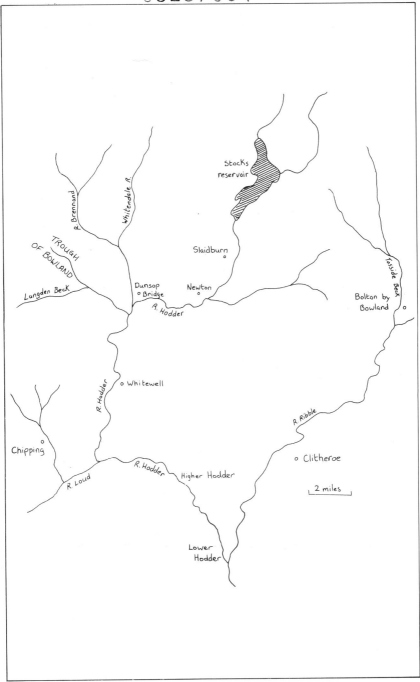

Stocks reservoir

R. Brennand

Whitendale R.

TROUGH OF BOWLAND

Langden Beck

Slaidburn o

Dunsop o Bridge

Newton o

R. Hodder

Tosside Beck

Bolton by Bowland o

o Whitewell

R. Hodder

R. Ribble

Chipping o

o Clitheroe

R. Loud

R. Hodder

Higher Hodder

2 miles

Lower Hodder

Bowland — An Introduction

"I go into Lancashire tomorrow, that part of the country lying beyond the mountains towards the western ocean. I go with a kind of dread, and trust in Divine providence".

So wrote William Camden (1551-1623) when contemplating a trip through the Trough of Bowland (pronounced Bolland) at the summit of which is an ancient stone marking the boundary between Lancashire and Yorkshire. Local folks would have had plenty to tell the intrepid traveller of the days of the Wars of the Roses when the two counties supported rivals for the throne of England. Around 15 miles from the stone and visible to the west on a clear day is the silvery ribbon of the Irish Sea whilst below to the east stretches the old county of Yorkshire. Bowland only became part of Lancashire in 1974. Camden's informants could doubtless have told him of the game which abounded in the surrounding forest when wolves, bears, wild cats and deer roamed free and the kings from Saxon times had jealously guarded their hunting grounds.

We must not imagine that the ancient forests of England were a mass of impenetrable trees and undergrowth. Bowland would certainly have had more trees than is the case today, but there would still have been open areas across which the deer would have been hunted as well as areas where they were allowed to "lie-up" and gather strength. The poor would dearly have loved to trap them here but were prevented from feeding their families on venison by savage forest laws. Strictly speaking Bowland was a chase rather than a forest. A chase requires only a few trees with open spaces between through which the hunt can pass easily. It was privately owned whereas a forest was totally owned by the king — in this sense Bowland was a chase.

The origin of the name Bowland as well as its precise boundaries have been the subject of debate, discussions at times being quite heated. Some workers suggest that it derives from 'the land of the cattle' but Ekwall suggests either a bow in a river or the land of the bow. Archery was certainly a long established tradition in these parts but the former explanation may well be the correct one. On the north side Bowland is bounded by the rivers Lune and Wenning whilst the sparkling waters of the Hodder mark its southern edge. To the east are the gritstone and flower-rich limestone escarpments whilst the Lancashire plain to the sea forms the western boundary. Within these boundaries Bowland and its famous Trough guarantee both historian and naturalist sights and sounds as fine as any in the land. This book offers ten gentle strolls to get the flavour of Bowland and its villages but you must sometimes get out your boots in order to cover greater distances. There are some problems which need to be overcome, particularly the lack of a regular bus service. Visitors arriving by car will also need to be aware of the lack of parking in some areas. Each of the chapters will therefore be based around a settlement with at least some chance of parking.

In 1964 when the Forest of Bowland was designated as an area of outstanding Natural Beauty, Pendle Hill was included within its 300 square miles of rolling moorland but from this book the Witch Country has been omitted having already been covered in the companion volume *"Exploring Pendle"* published in 1984.

The wild cat (above) and wolf (below) two of the animals which once roamed in the Forest of Bowland.

Chapter One
Around Bleasdale

Bleasdale Post Office – once a Smithy

Set into a hollow between the ancient markets of Garstang and Chipping, Bleasdale is a charming but tiny settlement surrounded by lovely fields and interesting buildings. I parked my car opposite the post office which also serves as a small cafe and bookshop. The building itself is a converted blacksmith's forge which must have been busy when the packhorse trains passed through. Looking at the building today it takes very little imagination to conjure up thoughts of a glowing forge — the sound of hot iron being struck, sparks flying, horses snorting and the Smith eager for news, quizzing the packhorse driver.

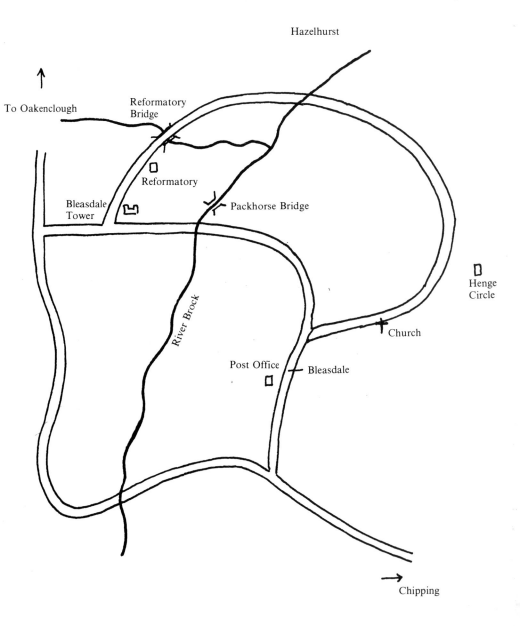

On the day of my last visit there was a hint of rain in the heavy air and swallows, swifts and house martins hawked low over the water of the Higher Brock stream which was overhung with hawthorn, alder and gorse and beneath these was a colourful tangle of summer flowers including late blooming bluebells, red campion and the white star-like blossoms of stitchwort.

A circular walk of around four miles leads from the post office, passing Bleasdale school and the church before sweeping across to a group of farms and an old reformatory before returning to the post office. Most visitors, however, may prefer to take two separate and more gentle strolls with a break for lunch and this is the pattern which I followed. Car owners will obviously find these two separate walks to be more logical.

Beyond the school and fringed by fields gleaming with golden buttercups I soon reached the parish church of St. Eadmer of Admarsh in Bleasdale, a pale coloured building looking much older than it really is. It was actually constructed in 1835 by John Dewhurst with an extensive addition being made to the chancel in 1897. It is the two west windows, however, which gives the feeling of antiquity and it is thought that these came from the Elizabethan church which the new structure replaced. An enquiry into the condition of this church in 1650 reported that it was in a sad state of repair. St. Eadmer was a religious writer of the 12th century so it may well be that a third church of even earlier date existed on the site.

Bleasdale's Parish Church

An even more ancient religion was practiced in the private fields beyond Vicarage farm. Here was sited a Wood Henge, now indicated by concrete filled holes whilst the few remnants have been removed to the Harris Museum in Preston for safe keeping. I often think that we do not take enough interest in the pre-historic sites of our part of England. There is no doubt that the Bleasdale Circle is an important site in a lovely setting below the slopes of Fairsnape fell. When illuminated by morning sunlight, scrapes on the fell known as 'sledge rows' are sometimes easily visible. These mark the route taken by loads of peat removed from the moorland to fire the hearths of Bleasdale and perhaps even the old smithy itself.

The Reformatory

After lunch I strolled a short distance along the road from Bleasdale towards Garstang before turning to the right along a beautiful leafy lane which eventually descended to a bridge over the evocatively named Baby Brock river. Beyond this 'new bridge' is a magnificent packhorse bridge set in a fairy-like dell, with ferns dripping from its span and the sweet smell of honeysuckle filling the air in late summer. The road continues to the Reformatory, built in 1857 by William James Garnett (1818-1873) who lived at Bleasdale Tower. Garnett set out to provide boys from Liverpool and Manchester, who had been in trouble, with a little discipline and a host of much needed skills including farming and shoemaking. The rather bleak building is however in a most delightful setting and provided some 30 boys with an environment which must have been better

The lovely black and white dipper is a feature of Bowland's fast running streams

than anything they had been accustomed to in the slums of the city. A short distance past the Reformatory is yet another bridge which was built by the lads themselves and it stands so strong today that it is a fitting tribute to the workers and, of course, their teachers. On one side is a plaque recording the boys' efforts and on the other is a series of carvings depicting the various tools used in the construction. The Reformatory building has now been converted into houses for the estate workers (the land is now owned by the Duckworth family) who still talk of Mr. Bullock the clogger who first came to Bleasdale as a city lad "in need of correction". A salutory tale is also told of 'difficult' characters being roped to a plough and used like horses to get rid of their excess energy.

The walk continues to a farm known as Hazelhurst which is the one remaining habitation in what was once a substantial settlement. During the 16th century almost 20 families lived under the shelter of Hazelhurst Fell and, judging by the presence of the stone supports of the stocks, not all were law abiding. There is always a sad feeling when standing in the centre of a deserted village and this is no exception. Huddled close to an ancient but healthy looking elm tree are a number of old buildings in varying stages of decay. I closed my eyes and conjured up the sound of pigs, hens, cattle lowing, the laughter and perhaps crying of children. I opened my eyes and looked at the 'sledge roads' up on Hazelhurst fells and marvelled at the toughness of folk who achieved self-sufficiency in these potentially inhospitable, if scenically beautiful, surroundings. The rain which had threatened all day now began to fall and somehow it seemed right to leave Hazelhurst in its own misty little hollow.

As I turned my back on the past and began the return journey to Bleasdale Post Office the sun managed to break through and reflected from the plumage of an albino pheasant, which was feeding along with many others of normal plumage being reared on the well-keepered estate. A dipper fed its young under the old packhorse bridge. It is surprising how local folk take their own countryside for granted. We are used to the perky, white-bibbed dipper along our streams but on this walk I was accompanied by a friend from the lowland south of England. Her excitement was intense as she watched the first dipper of her life! As we moved off rather suddenly we scared a woodpigeon which soon recovered and soared upwards and then produced a sharp cracking noise with its wings. This is the way the male displays to his mate.

This particular walk is one which proves that you do not have to scramble up steep paths or cover vast distances to strike into beautiful and lonely countryside. A look at the O.S. maps (Nos. 102, 103 and 98) will direct the energetic walker on a circular route from the church to Hazelhurst, the reformatory and return — a journey which should take about 4 hours allowing for stops.

Chapter Two
Around Chipping

St. Bartholomew's Church, Chipping – Viewed from the Car Park

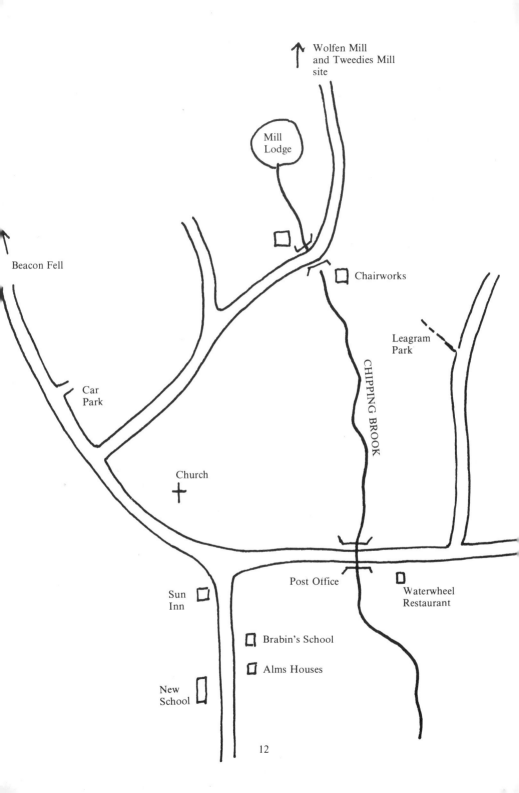

Wolfen Mill
and Tweedies Mill
site

Mill
Lodge

Beacon Fell

Chairworks

Leagram
Park

Car
Park

CHIPPING BROOK

Church

Post Office

Sun
Inn

Waterwheel
Restaurant

Brabin's School

Alms Houses

New
School

12

Anyone driving or walking around Bowland can be excused for thinking that all roads lead to Chipping. This ancient village was once an important market centre and it was therefore vital to mark the route to Chipping from every point of the compass. Whilst the 'bus service is not the most regular there is a large car park in the village and well-signed walks indicate gentle strolls into the heart of the Vale of Chipping. One of my favourites has the advantage of being circular and begins from the car park near the church and heads initially towards Parlick Pike. The energetic can follow the well-trodden route to the top and listen to the hill top birds including lapwing, curlew and golden plover. We have always envied birds the power of flight and an increasing number of intrepid hang gliders now hurl themselves from the slopes of Parlick and soar over the colourful meadows and patchwork patterns of the hamlets clustered around Chipping.

My favourite form of exercise is far more sedate and my route descends towards Berry's chairworks, a thriving concern utilising an old cotton mill situated opposite a group of fascinating old cottages which were once the village workhouse. I had chosen a splendid day and the hot sun was beating down from a clear blue sky as I crossed the bridge over Chipping Brook. Below the bridge is a flight of well worn steps which would have been essential to reach the stream in the days prior to piped water. All washing was done in the stream on the banks of which I found several healthy looking clumps of horsetails which are primitive plants related to the ferns and which once grew to heights of 50 feet (15.2 metres) when the climate of Britain was more tropical than it is today. In the Carboniferous period some 345 million years ago these swamp-loving plants were prolific, grew quickly but had a short life span. The weight of freshly dead plants crushed those beneath and eventually produced the 'fossil fuel' which we call coal. The climate is now too harsh and only a few of the smaller horsetails have managed to survive but in the not too distant past they were invaluable to the housewife. They contain a great deal of sand (silica) in their tissues and are therefore almost as rough as sandpaper. They were used as pan and pot scrubbers.

Despite the sometimes feverish and always fascinating activity at the chairworks it is almost worthwhile sitting in the vicinity with your eyes closed. Sounds of huge trees being sawn into workable planks, the whine of sanding machinery smoothing the wood and the clanking of the chains on the machinery never succeeds in swamping the calls of the birds in the nearby living trees, whilst the smell of sawdust and acetone-based varnishes almost — but not quite — overcome the scent of new-cut grass. Although Berry's is a go-ahead modern industry known world wide for the traditional design of its chairs the atmosphere of a rural, almost woodland based, industry remains inescapable.

At one time there were five water mills powered by Chipping Brook and apart from the chairworks another has been converted into a fine and popular restaurant sensibly called the Watermill. Wolfen Mill which once made bobbins and then functioned as a cheese factory was in a derelict condition and looked ready for demolition by the 1950s. It has now been tastefully converted into a residence of great charm and character. A footpath leads up to the old

Traditional chairs are still made in Chipping by Craftsmen   (Bill Wilkinson)

mill lodge which is popular with a variety of wildfowl. Whilst I was admiring the building a weasel eased its way, low slung and snake-like, out of a wall. It looked cheekily around to see what was going on and then twisted its way across the narrow road and vanished into a patch of nettles. These swayed when they were touched, disturbing a female small tortoiseshell butterfly which had been laying her eggs on the leaves.

Close to the mill lodge of Berry's chairworks and Wolfen Mill was Chipping Brook's more unusual mill, which has sadly been demolished. Tweedies began life as a cotton mill, but eventually earned a world wide reputation in maritime circles. How strange to find water turbines, portholes and other ship fitments being produced by craftsmen based so far inland.

Orders were received during the construction of Thomas Lupton's fine ship 'The Shamrock' and Tweedies mill was very busy up to the mid 1950s when shipbuilding began its sad decline. It is reasonable to suppose that inland "support factories" would be the first to suffer as everyone struggled to cut costs in order to remain competitive in a shrinking market. The mill has now gone and the derelict site is slowly being blanketed by bramble, thistles and the ubiquitous rosebay willow herb.

The winding road with its flower-strewn hedgerows twists and turns its way back into Chipping with its lovely old houses dominated by Saint Bartholomew's, one of the district's most beautiful churches. Chipping's own brook is actually a tributary of the river Loud and the valley must have been subject to regular flooding before effective drainage techniques evolved. The valley bottom must have been far too wet and unhealthy to support any permanent settlement. Malaria was a common disease of medieval Britain and the lowland swamps were a breeding ground for the blood sucking mosquitoes

Chipping Church which once dominated the market place – viewed from the main Street

15

which transmitted the disease from one person to another. For this reason the rocky knoll on which the church stands was ideal not only for St. Bartholomew's but also for the market. This combination of trade and religion was very common during this period. Look in the churchyard for the sundial dated 1708 but study the base carefully. This is probably part of the old market cross.

A church stood on this spot from at least AD 1041 but parts of the present building date from 1240. There were extensive additions and rebuilding in both the 15th and 16th centuries whilst the sturdy tower is dated at 1450. Extensive restoration was undertaken in 1873 but the overall shape of the building would seem not to have been significantly altered. There are Holy Water stoupes scattered throughout the interior of the church and a Piscina which was part of the original 12th century church. The font has been dated to 1520 and is thought to have been given by the Bradley family whose initials are carved on one of several shields around the font. Other carvings show details of Christ's Passion. Easily distinguishable are nails, scourges, hammer and pincers. Two blank shields are something of a mystery, but there are signs that the original carvings were removed. This may have been the doings of a zealous Puritan and some historians have suggested that they were carvings of the Five Wounds of Christ or perhaps the Holy Heart. The "Saxon runes" which are carved around the base might not have survived if the Puritans had stood on their heads and discovered that these were not runes but inverted initials which read A M G P D T. This is thought to relate to a section from the gospel of St. Luke chapter one verse 28: *Ave Maria Gratia Plena Dominus Tocum* which translates as *Hail Mary thou that art highly favoured, the Lord is with thee.*

The Shireburn family were influential in Bowland for many centuries but are usually remembered for their magnificent house at Stoneyhurst and the family tombs in Great Mitton church. Chipping was also influenced by the family and there was once a Shireburn chantry here which was also known as the Wolfhouse Quire referring to the family home at Wolfen Hall. Chantries had far too many Roman Catholic overtones for the Puritans and often were ripped out with a complete disregard for damage done to the fabric of the building. All that remains of the old chantry is a Holy Water stoupe, but it was sited close to the Berry Memorial window. This lovely piece of modern stained glass commemorates the life of the founder of the chairworks. The original function of stained glass in churches was to tell a story in pictures to those who were unable to read. They were thus the original visual aid used by priests who were also the medieval teaching profession. It is always good to see the tradition maintained and looking at the Berry window it is easy to study the art of chair making. Another of the Church's functions was to assist in healing the sick either using faith or medicine. It is interesting to read the list of Chipping's rectors beginning with Robert in AD 1230 who was followed ten years later by Peter the Physician.

If the visitor descends the steps from the churchyard and turns left the real beauty of the village is soon appreciated. We must pause by the gates, however, and relate an interesting story which unfolds when a wedding party is leaving after the ceremony. Known as "Perrying", the local children secure the gate

The Village Abattoir at Chipping, until recently part of the butcher's shop

with rope and refuse to open it until coins are thrown down the steps and which are scrambled for with a surprisingly fierce determination.

The first village shop reached is the old butcher's house now closed and replaced by a modern complex at the top of the village. By the side of the old shop is a narrow alleyway down which the animals were driven from the back and were unable to turn before entering the slaughter house. In Old English the word "Chipping" meant market and the butcher's shop with its attached abattoir is just one example of how self contained it must have been. Down the narrow, well-named Windy Street where there always seems to be a breeze, to Brabin's (or Brabyn's) school built with money given by a Quaker benefactor who died in 1683. John Brabin made his fortune as a dyer and cloth dealer. On Talbot Street, the main thoroughfare of the village, is the post office and craft shop. A plaque on the wall informs us that here was Brabin's shop, office and home. The old school is now used as a youth club and a new building still carrying his name is attended by the local children receiving their primary education. It is rather nice to think of the blue coated Brabin scholars trudging down the street to meet their master who lived in an adjacent house, also provided by the founder. High standards were set and in his will Brabin ordered that any master falling short was to be instantly "put out" by the governors.

John Brabin's School, Chipping

18

Chipping's Main Street. The post office, once Brabin's home, is seen on the far left

No visit to Chipping would be complete without a gentle stroll past the Watermill restaurant, turning left towards Leagram. If the bridlepath around 1½ miles from Chipping and signed to Stanley is followed for a short distance it takes us backwards in time into the surrounds of Leagram Hall, surely some of the most magnificent rolling parkland to be found anywhere in Britain. Leagram began as a medieval deer park, but many of the splendid trees, including ash and oak, would probably have been known to the owner John Weld who was a fine naturalist and who kept detailed diaries of his observations between 1850 and 1886. In September 1856 he reported a swallow which was "dull white without a single coloured feather about it, the eye was black with a beautiful bright yellow rim encircling it".

During my stroll through the park I sought shelter from the broiling sun beneath a spreading ash and looked in vain for a white swallow among the large number swooping low over the fields full of cattle. The birds were obviously catching the flies which were attracted to the cow pats. Far too soon it was time to return to Chipping set in an area which never fails to delight the naturalist and historian alike. It handles its visitors well and never loses the air of old world serenity.

Chapter Three
Around Whitewell

Whitewell Hotel with the chapel on the left

When is a forest not a forest? As we saw in the introduction, we think of a huge expanse of trees with a tangle of undergrowth, but to our Saxon ancestors the forest was a place to hunt wild beasts including wolves, wild boar, pine martens and of course deer. When the invading Normans took over the forests there were obviously plenty of trees but there were also large open areas across which they could hunt. Two of the best gallops were within the forests of Rossendale and Bowland. Many of Bowland's trees have now been felled; there has been a lot of replanting in recent years although conifers have predominated. The walk from Whitewell to Cow Ark enables us to understand how the old forest was managed.

Whitewell was the old administrative centre of the forest, the chief officer being a master forester and his deputy was known as the bow bearer. Before the building of the inn at Whitewell, a lodge existed and functioned as a combination between an office and a courtroom. Peasants could be punished for the offences of venison (killing deer) and vert (cutting down timber). They were only allowed to take small branches for their fires and only those rotting branches which they could reach using a hook or a crook. Here we have the origin of the phrase "By hook or by crook", when we speak of reaching an objective.

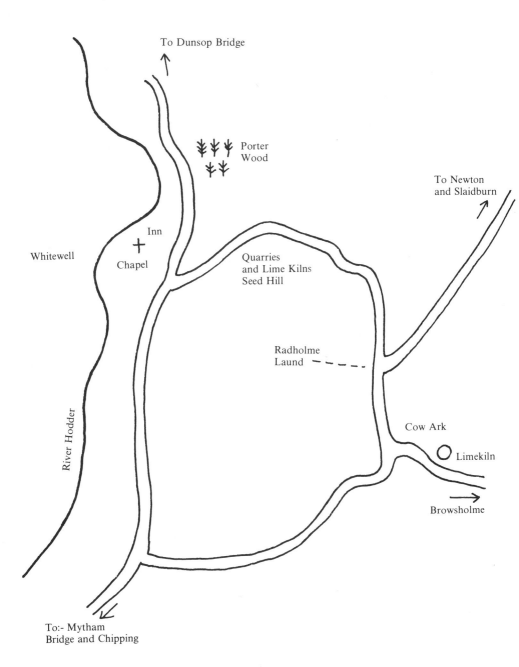

To Dunsop Bridge

Porter Wood

To Newton and Slaidburn

Inn

Whitewell

Chapel

Quarries and Lime Kilns Seed Hill

Radholme Laund

Cow Ark

River Hodder

Limekiln

Browsholme

To:- Mytham Bridge and Chipping

21

Two fine examples of Lime Kilns

Whitewell's chapel began in 1422 as a chapel of ease in which a corpse from a distant place could be deposited for the night on its way for burial in a properly consecrated church. Whitewell church is now administered from Chipping. In 1836, the church of St. Michael was rebuilt and is now overlooked by a lime tree which produces so much nectar that it seems to be full of drunken bees during the summer and early autumn. Inside the church is a fine Flemish tapestry on loan from Browsholme Hall. The Whitewell Inn provides a welcome for the walkers and for fishermen who find good sport in the River Hodder which bends around Whitewell. This is one of the finest salmon and trout stretches in the north west.

The stroll to Cow Ark begins with a stiff climb up Hall Hill and in the heat of a summer's day I was more than glad to make use of a seat provided in memory of John and Mary Edwards. This had been sensibly sited at the summit overlooking a quarry and a disused lime kiln was being used by a pair of pied wagtails and a pair of pigeons to raise their hungry families, whose cries echoed around the arches of the building. Many folk prefer to drive this route and there are a few handy spots to pull in and look out over the magnificent scenery.

The quarry, long disused, contains many fascinating fossils, including sea lilies, showing that this part of Bowland was once submerged beneath shallow sea. As Bowland changed gradually from a forest to an agricultural society, the quarry must have been vital for building material and for the lime to neutralise the natural acidity of the soil.

A look at the map, however, will take us back to the forest. A farm known as Radholme Laund refers to its origins as a deer enclosure, while just beyond is another farm called Park Gate which was obviously just that. Both native Red and the lovely spotted Fallow deer, probably introduced by the Normans, were emparked here.

From the early 15th century, deer became less and less important, and the Parkers of Browsholme were becoming prominent and switching their allegiance from deer to cattle.

Cow Ark, now a pretty but insignificant settlement, reflects this change in land use. Opposite the telephone box is a finger post informing us that we are six miles from Clitheroe, 19½ miles from Lancaster and three miles from Whitewell.

On the day of my walk, rain during the night had been followed by a hot morning and in conditions like this the scents of plants carry over a wide area. The ramsons near the river bottom under the bridge at Cow Ark fill the valley with the strong smell of garlic. Further along the road back to Hall Hill a strong smell of aniseed enabled me to find a relative of the carrot family which is called sweet cecily. Meadow sweet, a member of the rose family, added its heady sweetness and I also found water mint in a damp hedge. Colour, if not aroma, was added by the deep blue of germander speedwell and the shining yellow of silverweed. One discovery, however, took me straight back to the old forest of Bowland. This was a patch of dogs mercury. This plant spreads very slowly and only grows in woods. What was it doing miles away from woodlands? It is what botanists call an indicator species and tells us that the area was once covered in trees. We know it was but it is nice to have it proved.

Chapter Four
Bashall Town and Eaves

Only just visible, a lovely old Packhorse Bridge between Bashall Town and Eaves, now fringed and overhung with trees

I once met a walker armed with a map and a most confused expression on her face. She had left her car in the village of Waddington to go in search of Bashall Town, but had failed to find anything but a lovely old hall and a cluster of farms. She had continued to Bashall Eaves and knew that Eaves meant a settlement on the edge of a wood. It is easy to understand that a wood can disappear but what about the town? What has happened around Bashall?

The area was at one time under the control of the Talbot family and a substantial hamlet was concentrated around the splendid old Tudor Hall. Behind the privately owned architectural jewel is a barn-like building known as the retainers' dwelling which is unique in the north west. It is a reminder of

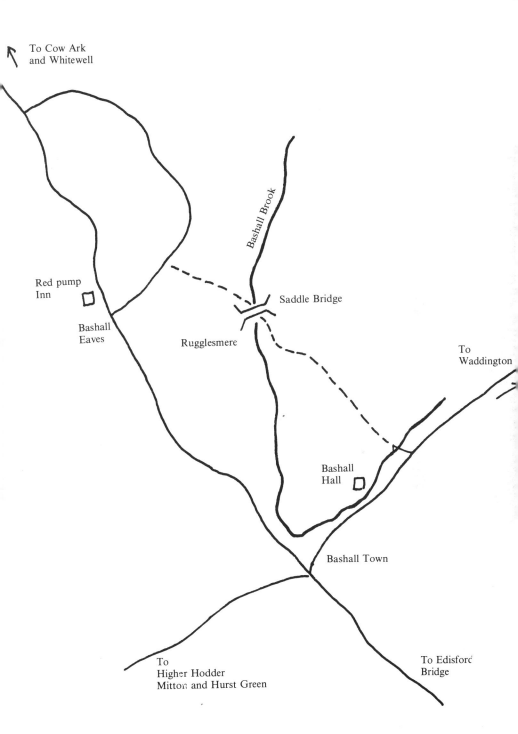

To Cow Ark
and Whitewell

Bashall Brook

Red pump
Inn

Saddle Bridge

Bashall
Eaves

Rugglesmere

To
Waddington

Bashall
Hall

Bashall Town

To
Higher Hodder
Mitton and Hurst Green

To Edisford
Bridge

Bashall Hall – one of Bowland's most delightful and historic houses

just how dangerous life was at the time of the Wars of the Roses. Bashall was then in Yorkshire but perilously close to Lancashire with the river Ribble serving as the boundary. The wars split families and many, like the Talbots, found it prudent to maintain their own small army and the retainers' dwelling is really an example of a 15th century barracks. Bashall Eaves was then on the outskirts of a settlement substantial enough in the context of the period to be called a town. Beyond the Eaves was the forest and it is only in recent times that the two have been linked by a modern road. Is there any evidence of the medieval route? Indeed there is. A footpath leads from Bashall to Bashall Eaves via Saddle Bridge. This is a single span packhorse bridge with a sweeping high arch looping over a stream on which dippers and grey wagtails breed. The bridge is overhung and at times almost obscured by the branches of alder, elm and hawthorn. The cobbles of the old highway can occasionally be felt underfoot, the line of the route being more easily deliniated when etched with an early morning frost and illuminated by the first rays of the sun. From Rugglesmere Farm beyond the bridge the path leads between high hedges which include many species of tree including hawthorn, oak, rowan, mountain ash and some very high hollies. This tells us that this hedge has been long established because holly trees grow very slowly, have a long life span and some specimens hereabouts are almost 60 feet (18.3 metres) in height. Early winter is an ideal time to undertake this walk and it will be noticed that not all the hollies have berries. This is because the holly is an example of a dioecious plant with the

26

Browsholme Hall

It is fascinating to see how many pieces were removed from Whalley Abbey (above) to be incorporated into the structure of such fine buildings as Browsholme Hall

female flowers carried on a separate plant to the male flowers. Obviously only the female trees bear berries. Those buying holly trees from the garden centres need to be very aware of this fact, and choose their plants during the "berry season".

The hedgerow is also interesting in the summer when a short search will reveal a wide variety of flowers. In late June I found bluebells still in flower as well as barren strawberry, crosswort, stitchwort and bistort. The latter is most attractive to look at but its scent is far from pleasant and its country name of sweaty sock plant is well deserved. Later in the year honeysuckle will perfume the route and pollinating bees can be seen crawling eagerly into the purple bells of the foxglove.

The life of a packhorse journeyman would have been most unpleasant on days of driving snow, freezing rain or in fog when the reason for placing bells around the necks of the horses becomes obvious. But what about travelling through these leafy lanes and over crystal clear streams on a warm summer's day with birds singing from a hawthorn weighed down with white, heavily perfumed blossom. I don't see much stress here — only a feeling of job satisfaction.

Both the old Bashall route and the modern road head in the direction of the home of the Parkers who were the traditional bowbearers (legal administrators) of the Forest of Bowland. The old route takes us via a narrow path known locally as "Rabbit Lane". Rabbits certainly did not represent free grub for local folk but were fiercely protected by land owners. Rabbits, formerly called coneys, are not native to this country but were introduced by the Normans as a luxury food and were guarded by an estate worker called the Warrener. Not only were the peasants not allowed to eat rabbits but strict laws were in force to prevent folk from chasing the hungry beasts away from their crops! It was certainly the rich "wot got the gravy and the poor wot got the blame" in the early history of the British rabbit! It was only when agriculture became more efficient during the 18th and 19th centuries that the rabbits could pinch enough food to increase rapidly and break out of their warrens to become an economic pest but it was well into the 19th century before their traditional protection was lifted.

The energetic walker or those using a car should complete their day by continuing towards Browsholme Hall which is open on summer Sundays from 2 p.m. to 5 p.m. and at other times by appointment. The Parker family have lived here since the 14th century and the present hall was built in 1507 but refaced in attractive red sandstone in 1604. The gardens are a riot of summer colour whilst within are a few priceless pieces of stained glass removed from Whalley Abbey when it was dissolved in 1537. With regard to the history of the Forest of Bowland perhaps the most fascinating item in Browsholme is a gauge which was once used to measure dogs. Nobody without due authority was allowed to keep a dog large enough to hunt deer. Animals which would not pass through the gauge were deemed too large and either had to be killed or have their legs mutilated so that they could not pursue the deer. The pace of medieval life was so much more leisurely than is the case today but how cruel it must have seemed to be at times!

Chapter Five
Stocks Reservoir

St. James' Church, Dalehead

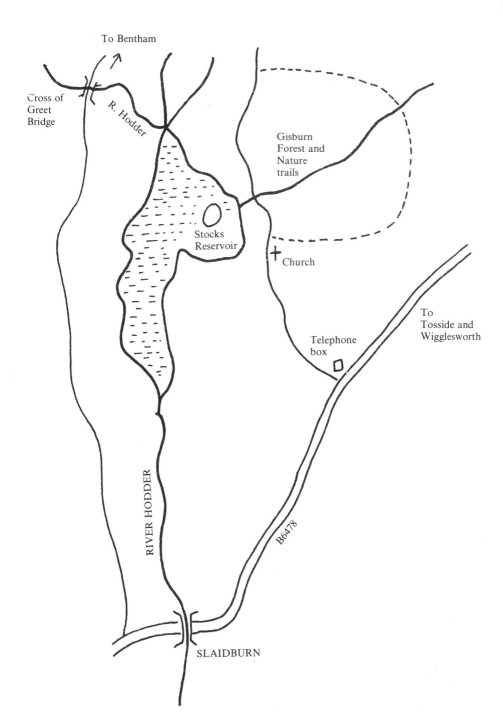

To Bentham

Cross of
Greet
Bridge

R. Hodder

Gisburn
Forest and
Nature
trails

Stocks
Reservoir

✝ Church

Telephone
box

To
Tosside and
Wigglesworth

RIVER HODDER

B6478

SLAIDBURN

The infant waters of the River Hodder once flowed along a pebbled bed through the village of Stocks, which should perhaps be more accurately referred to as Dale Head. I descended from the highlands above Tosside and felt the full force of the north easterly wind which whipped ice into my face and each angled piece of hail brought its own sharp sting. There did seem the chance of a clear spell of weather and I was glad to find temporary sanctuary from the elements in St. James' Church at Dalehead which thankfully I found to be open. I took off my gloves and blew hard on my hands to restore some circulation. What a contrast this was from my previous visit on a steamy hot and sticky day when the churchyard smelled of freshly cut grass and the borders were strewn with wild flowers including both marsh and common spotted orchids, red common sorrel, bright yellow tormentil and the more delicate shades of lady's mantle. But January weather in these high places is altogether different and I found myself eagerly longing for the warmth of a cottage or an inn's log fire blazing in the hearth. Alas Dalehead can no longer provide such a luxury as a glance at a rather forlorn notice on the wall of the church bears witness. It tells us that not far from the present church the old village lies submerged beneath the waters of the Fylde Water Boards reservoir. There were once some twenty houses, a shop, post office and a pub called 'The New Inn'. Stand on the road and look out over the water towards the grassy island which in summer echoes to the strident calls of breeding black headed gulls. The village lay just to the right of the island and in times of severe drought some of the old buildings can be seen. A few foundations can be seen on the edge of the 'lake'. The Fylde Water Board Act of 1925 sealed the fate of the village and the demolition of the buildings began. On November 12th 1926 the Bishop of Bradford consecrated a new burial ground above the water level and on 30th July 1938 the present church was consecrated having been built with stone from the original church. This was not very old only being consecrated in 1852. Evensong is held every third Sunday which always reminds me of a mellow October evening when I had been bird watching and the sound of Canada geese returning to their roost mingled with the gentle refrain of a hymn. I closed my eyes and gave a silent prayer for the old folks of Dalehead and wondered how many tears they shed as they watched the waters rising against the new dam and swamping their homes, church and pub. Think how you would feel if forced to watch your home drowned!

If the villagers returned they would not recognise very much of the surrounding scenery. The Forestry Commission has also been active and has clothed the hillsides with conifers although some native trees and shrubs remain including birch, alder, hazel and dog roses. At one time the Commission was most reluctant to allow visitors into its plantations but in recent years this attitude has mellowed. Parking spaces are provided and well designed nature walks penetrate the forest and climb to some delightful scenic picnic spots. The trails have even been graded. The red trail takes an estimated 75 minutes in contrast to the strolls of 50 minutes along the white route and a gentle 40 minutes following the blue arrows. At Hollins Bay a day permit for fishing may be obtained, but it is the naturalist, especially the winter bird watcher, who has most to gain from a visit to Stocks. The strength of the site is its variety of

Reed Bunting
Male (Top) Female (Bottom)

Crossbill

Sparrowhawks breed in the conifers of Gisburn Forest

habitat. From the trails panoramic views over the 344-acre reservoir can reveal winter flocks of Canada geese, tufted duck, pochard, mallard, teal, wigeon and goldeneye. Birds of prey include sparrowhawk, kestrel, tawny and long eared owl plus rarities such as osprey, goshawk and hen harrier. The reservoir is surrounded by the 4000 acres of Gisburn Forest which, although quite dense, can often reward careful watchers with sightings of woodcock, raven, redstart and barn owl with flocks of crossbills occasionally passing through in autumn. Above the trees on the rolling moorland short eared owl and both black and red grouse are seen along with the more common species such as skylarks, meadow pipits and wheatears.

The area has been made much more accessible since the new car parks and paths have been opened and most of the walks are very gentle whilst the serious walker can find more strenuous exercise by following one of several tracks over the Bowland Fells.

Chapter Six
Around Longridge and Jeffrey Hill

Club Row, Longridge

Parking my car in Longridge I prepared for the uphill stroll onto the breezy heights of Jeffrey Hill. For those short of wind the route can still be followed by car because it sticks to the road. The reason for this road being chosen is that a row of houses has a fascinating tale to tell. Way back in 1793 a group of twenty men formed themselves into a club to which they each struggled to pay one guinea (£1.05) each month. This was used to purchase materials towards the construction of a cottage which was to have both a "necessary and a coal house". The men themselves provided the labour during their limited amount of free time. When a house was completed a ballot was organised by the local vicar and the lucky winner moved in. The process continued until all the original twenty were housed in what has become known as Club Row. This early example of a building society proved very popular and a similar arrangement was undertaken in other villages including Chipping. Longridge's houses still stand surprisingly fresh looking and a sign of modern prosperity is the line of cars parked along Club Row.

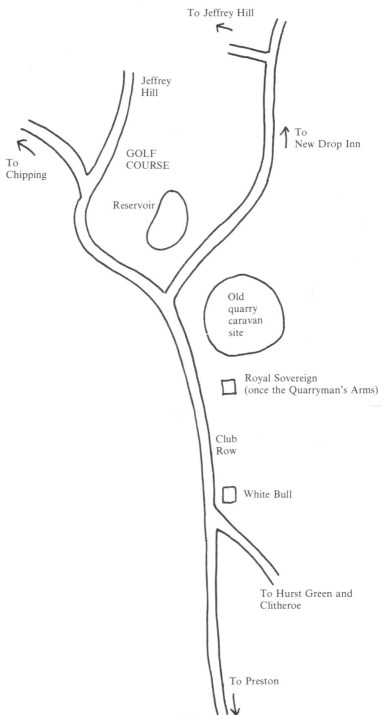

To Jeffrey Hill

Jeffrey
Hill

GOLF
COURSE

To
New Drop Inn

To
Chipping

Reservoir

Old
quarry
caravan
site

Royal Sovereign
(once the Quarryman's Arms)

Club
Row

White Bull

To Hurst Green and
Clitheroe

To Preston

35

Royal Sovereign, Longridge

Further up the hill is another intriguing building bearing the name 'Royal Sovereign' with the date 1808 easily visible against the background of the hotel's white walls. Also seen above the date are what appears to be a set of strange hieroglyphics. It is only when we find that the pub was once called 'The Quarryman's Arms' that we realise that we are looking at the tools of that tough trade in the days before mechanisation put brain where there had previously been only strength, muscle and acquired skill. At one side of the building a bridle path leads towards Blackburn road whilst on the other side is the entrance to a caravan site. This has been sited within the artistically landscaped disused Tootle quarry. From here came the stone for the construction of Liverpool Docks when the port was expanding rapidly during the 19th century. Tootle quarrystone also went to Preston for the construction of St. Walburge's church and the Harris library.

Still climbing steeply and twisting its way alongside a reservoir I found the fresh moorland breeze a welcome relief from the heat of the valley and I paused to eat my lunch in a gateway. The rushy fields echoed to the cries of curlews and the lapwings and the well named cotton grass bobbed about in the wind, like thousands of rabbits' tails. After lunch I continued my steady climb past Longridge Golf Club and eventually reached my objective — the top of Jeffrey Hill. A number of cars were parked and their passengers were enjoying a picnic overlooking the vale of Chipping whilst away to the left the sparkling sea washing the Fylde coast can be seen like a silver ribbon. The straight line of the old Roman road can also be seen as can Fell, fringed with trees and dwarfed by the bulk of Parlick. Both were probably beacon hills, but I find the explanation of the origin of Parlick given by some workers rather puzzling. 'Pyre' from a funeral pile and 'lick' referring to the flames of the fire seems a little trite. In his 'Place names of Lancashire' David Mills suggests the name means a pear tree enclosure from the Old English words Pirige and loc. In 1228 it was written Perlak. I prefer the explanation given by Ekwall in his "the Concise Oxford Dictionary of English Place Names". He suggests the derivation is from pharra which means either a parish, district or enclosure. This sounds a much more logical explanation.

The fields below Jeffrey Hill seemed full of cattle chewing contentedly in the sunshine and as I also enjoyed a rest amongst the heather I noticed that the bilberries were already beginning to ripen. I could hear a whitethroat singing from a thorn tree and a family of tiny rabbits were scampering about in the undergrowth. Among the flowers was a lovely carpet of blue germander speedwell and white deadnettle. The latter, as its name implies, does not sting and is in fact, not a nettle at all but a member of the square stemmed family called the Labiatae. In some country districts the flowers are called 'Adam and Eve'. To see why, look under the upper lip of the corolla (this is the group name for the petals) and you will find two black and yellow stamens lying side by side. They do look like two naked human figures without even a fig leaf between them! Many folk never dare risk this peep into nature's innermost secrets because they cannot believe that anything with leaves so like those of a nettle is actually 'dead' and cannot possibly sting.

Once more a stroll through our northern countryside has revealed a blend of history, natural history, folk lore, fact and fiction. An old mill worker once said to me "Thee get aht into yon hills lad. There is nowt to lick it ahm telling thee".

All I can say is that "Ee were reet".

There is one good thing about walking up to Jeffrey Hill — its a very easy stroll back down into Longridge!

A female woodmouse, common mammal in Bowland　　　　　*[Mick Chesworth]*

Razor Strop Fungus

Chapter Seven
Beacon Fell

Larch – grows well on Beacon Fell

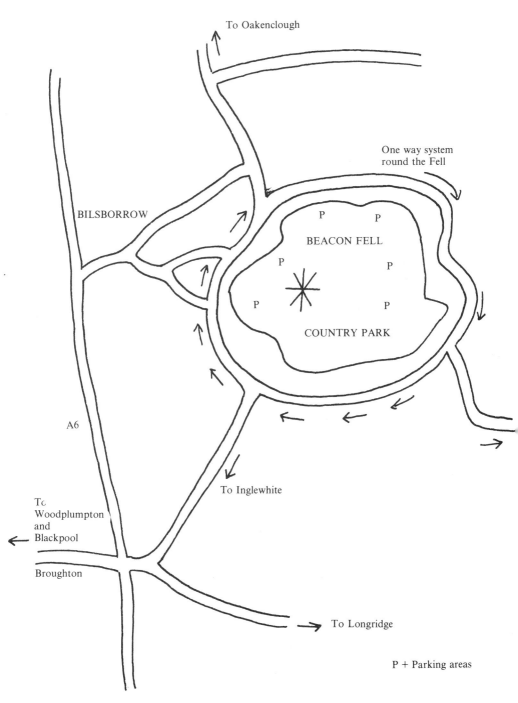

To Oakenclough

One way system
round the Fell

BILSBORROW

P   P

BEACON FELL

P   P

P   P

COUNTRY PARK

A6

To Inglewhite

To
Woodplumpton
and
Blackpool

Broughton

To Longridge

P + Parking areas

41

Although Beacon Fell is only 873 feet (266 metres) its mainly conifer clad summit dominates the plain of West Lancashire, with Blackpool clearly visible on a good day whilst to the east Bowland is laid out in all its splendour. No wonder it has been used as one of a chain of beacon hills since the Bronze Age. By lighting fires on the summits vital signals could be transmitted with surprising speed. Those of us who walk the hills, however, know only too well that we can suffer for days on end under heavy rain and low swirling clouds. Invading forces would quickly have learned to attack during periods of poor visibility.

Beacon Fell has now been designated as a country park and spread among its 273 acres are numerous car parks and a visitors' centre is usually open at weekends although unfortunately not during the week. Very sensibly a one way system for cars has been marked along the narrow road which spirals its way to the summit. Whilst the majority of trees around the fell are commercially grown conifers there are many native species including oak, ash, rowan and silver birch. Among the conifers are spruce, pine and larch. There is a simple way of distinguishing between the three. All you have to do is to try to pull off a leaf. Spruce leaves come off singly, pine leaves break off in pairs whilst the larch leaves come away in lumps. Thus we have S for spruce and single, P for pine and pair and L for both larch and lump! This is a rough and ready rule but it works most of the time. Two sorts of spruce are grown commercially and are sold as Christmas trees. Norway spruce is the European species although it never occurs naturally in Britain. Its foliage is soft and both the upper and lower surfaces of the leaves are bright green. These are ideal for Christmas trees whilst the foliage of the sitka spruce from North America (Sitka is a town in Canada) is green on top, grey green beneath and is very prickly. Next time you buy your tree ask for Norway spruce and you will find it much more comfortable to decorate!

This mixture of trees encourages a rich and varied wildlife to Beacon fell. The majority of visitors, however, arrive in the middle of the day when the birds and beasts are having a quiet siesta but those who can arrive early and leave late will have much more to observe. I arrived just as the sun was rising and the pink flush of dawn was providing a soft blush over Bowland. Without getting out of the car I wound down the window and had a quiet cup of coffee and a cold bacon sandwich. Out of the undergrowth came a long tailed field mouse which ran along a dead moss-covered branch. Also known as the woodmouse this attractive creature can climb trees every bit as well as a squirrel and also uses its long tail to help it to balance. A grunting, snuffling noise indicated that a hedgehog was taking a late breakfast before seeking out a comfortable spot in which to sleep out the day.

Even though it was towards the end of June the sound of the birds coming to life was dramatic, and among the choir I recognised song thrush, blackbird, robin, wren, blackcap and willow warbler. A cock pheasant called loudly and cattle and sheep joined in from the fields below to welcome the new day. A treecreeper worked its way spirally up an old birch covered with bracket fungus. This used to be called the razor strop fungus because it was so tough and

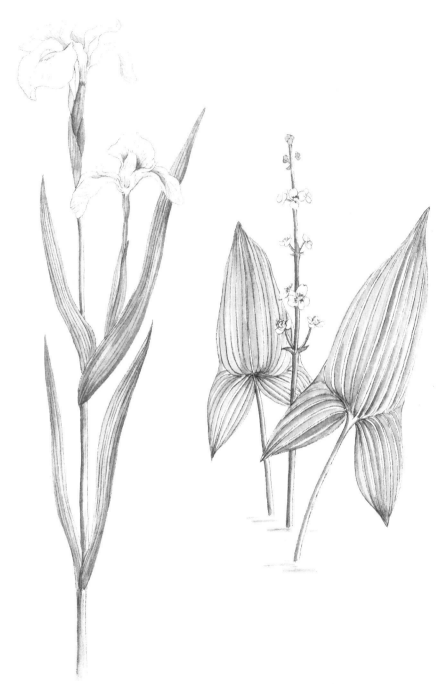

Two of Bowland's riverside flowers – yellow Flag (left) Arrowhead (right)

Small tortoishell butterfly feeding on nettles

rubbery that it was used to sharpen the old cut throat razors and also the bill hooks which were used when laying hedges and cutting through vegetation. Sunlight was slinking through a patch of nettles and a red admiral was spreading wide its wings to catch every ray of heat. Butterflies are cold blooded and the cooler they are the slower they move and are therefore more vulnerable to predators. They therefore spend the early morning soaking up the sun which is their equivalent to a Grand Prix driver revving up prior to the start of the race.

Beacon Fell also has its share of interesting plants including blackberries and cranberries which attract late summer and autumn visitors fired with a desire to live off the land. Around the fell are a number of small ponds in which grow yellow flag and arrowhead, the latter so named because of the shape of its leaves. Gerard, the 16th century herbalist, called it the water archer but did not recommend it as a cure for any illness. This is surprising because it was a plant recommended by those who practiced the Doctrine of Signatures. This meant that God had put His sign on each and every plant to tell us what they could be used for. Those wounded by an arrow were therefore ritualistically dosed with a brew made by dropping nine dried leaves of arrowhead into hot water. The fact that Gerard, who was very skilled for the age in which he lived, did not include it in his herbal suggests that it was useless.

Beacon Fell has many virtues but the good parking and well marked paths so rich in wildlife all combine to ensure a regular flow of visitors. Despite this the cover given by the trees can give the feeling of being alone despite the close proximity of other visitors.

Chapter Eight
Slaidburn and Newton

St. Andrew's, Slaidburn

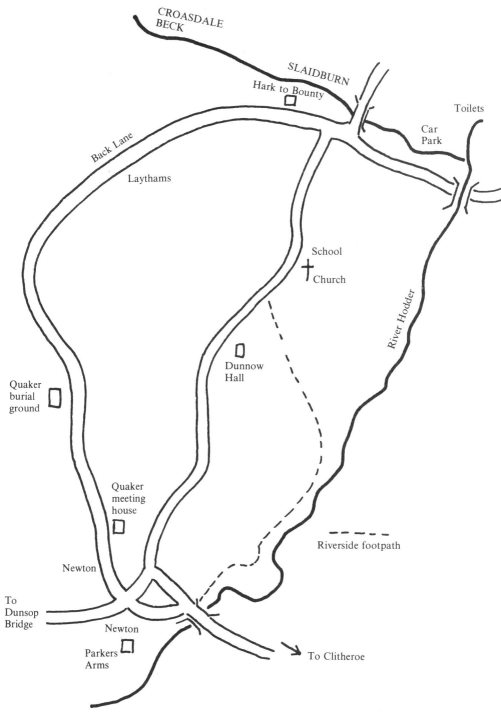

CROASDALE BECK

SLAIDBURN

Hark to Bounty

Toilets

Car Park

Back Lane

Laythams

School

Church

River Hodder

Quaker burial ground

Dunnow Hall

Quaker meeting house

Newton

Riverside footpath

To Dunsop Bridge

Newton

Parkers Arms

To Clitheroe

Slaidburn's famous old Inn 'Hark to Bounty'

There can be no better walk than the one connecting these two beautiful and historic villages. This gentle stroll has the added bonus of following the meanderings of the Hodder, one of the prettiest and least polluted of any river in Britain. There is only one fault — a single day is hardly sufficient to appreciate what is on offer.

Slaidburn has two fine bridges one spanning the Hodder and the other its tributary, Croasdale Beck, which is almost as substantial as the main stream itself. A lovely, gently rising footpath follows Croasdale Beck through pretty woodland and a former corn mill can be seen from Jubilee gardens with the mill leet and pond both clearly visible. Rabbit breeding was once one of the village industries, the pelts being used for making hats. The main car park is below the village and alongside the Hodder with its graceful bridge carrying traffic towards Stocks in Bowland and Tosside. A stroll back into the village leads past a tea shop and a fine war memorial to one of Bowland's most famous inns. Hark to Bounty until 1861 was known as the plain Dog Inn but it is then alleged that whilst the Master of the Hunt was taking refreshment he heard his favourite dog eager to continue the sport and he said "Just Hark to Bounty" and the name stuck. When the old court house was demolished local justice was meted out at the Hark to Bounty. A window at the rear of the pub and studded with coloured glass is probably a remnant of the old court, the site of which is still remembered in the name of a field — Court House Close. There was once a second pub in the village on the corner almost opposite Hark to Bounty, named the Black Bull but this is now used as a Youth Hostel. The start of the gentle stroll to the village of Newton begins at the church of St. Andrew parts of which were constructed as early as the 12th century but it is on the site of an even earlier settlement. The name Slaidburn probably means a sheep field overlooking a river. This description is still true today and a look across at the sloping fields adjacent to the church will reveal a number of cultivation terraces called lynchets which were typical of Anglo-Saxon agriculture. The tower of the church is a mighty structure which seems to have provided protection during the Scots' raids of 1322 when their confidence was sky high after Bruce's victory at Bannockburn in the same year. Outside in the churchyard is a sundial the base of which, as at Chipping might well be part of the old market cross. Once more we see Church and commerce working together. A third facet is also evident in Slaidburn — education. The old Grammar school has a date stone of 15 May 1717 which records the generosity of a farmer named John Brennand, who funded its construction. Attached to this historic building are the modern extensions of the village junior school. There are two road routes from Slaidburn to Newton but the footpath along the river is one of the finest strolls in Bowland.

On this stroll I have a favourite tree — a gnarled old alder. Late in April I watched a kingfisher perched on an overhanging bough looking hopefully into a deep pool. In November the tree seemed alive with siskins and long tailed tits feeding greedily on the seeds. In the old days the alder trees were 'farmed' by the clog sole makers who fashioned the footwear from the alder. What better timber to use for long lasting clogs in a damp climate than that from a tree which grows with its feet in water! This path does get quite muddy after rain, however, and so it is at its best on a hot day in late summer with the smell of hay being made and the sound of crickets chirping. Their mating calls are an excellent substitute for car fumes and traffic noise on the main roads leading to and from the tourist traps. The well marked route soon reaches Newton Bridge from which a short cut climb leads to the Parker's Arms with its beer garden and on into the village of Newton itself. There has probably been a settlement here since

Clogger using Alder Wood

Roman times as it is on their road from Lancaster through Wigglesworth and then on to York. There are no remains of this settlement though and neither is there a church — it is close enough to be in the parish of Slaidburn. There is, however, an historic Quaker's Meeting House built in 1767 and where Newton's residents once educated their sons thanks to the generosity of John Brabin, a philanthropist we have already met. John Bright, the politician who was so influential in repealing the Corn Laws in the 1830s, was a pupil of the Quaker school. As the road climbs out of Newton the meeting house is on the right and the burial ground fringed by trees is on the left. This road leads back to Slaidburn by eventually following the line of Croasdale Beck via Laythams. The whole journey can be covered in a short day with a break for lunch and without raising too much of a sweat. There are also a number of well signed short cuts across the fields.

Chapter Nine
Bolton by Bowland

The Brown Hare is a common animal in Bowland, despite its persecution

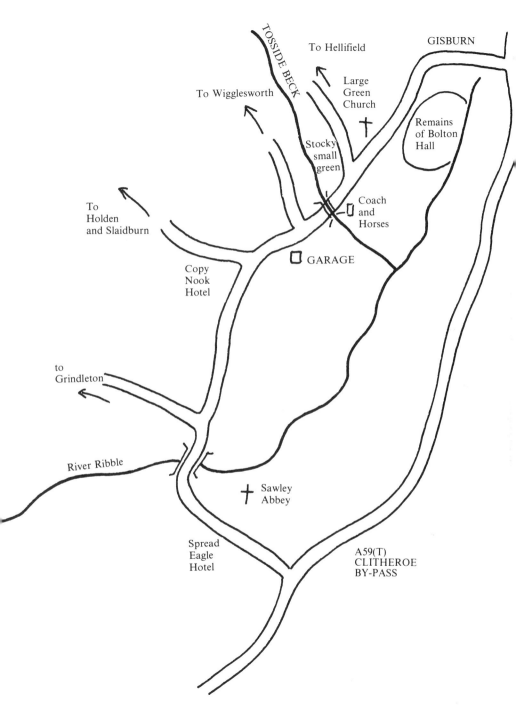

TOSSIDE BECK

GISBURN

To Hellifield

Large
Green
Church

To Wigglesworth

Remains
of Bolton
Hall

Stocky
small
green

To
Holden
and Slaidburn

Coach
and
Horses

GARAGE

Copy
Nook
Hotel

to
Grindleton

River Ribble

Sawley
Abbey

Spread
Eagle
Hotel

A59(T)
CLITHEROE
BY-PASS

Rain pelted down from an iron grey sky and swept down from the church into the usually peaceful village of Bolton by Bowland. How can I forget my first visit some years ago when weather and the harriers of hares shattered the peace? Steam rose from horses, cold wet hunters reached down from the saddle to pick up their stirrup cups brimming with warming beverage, dogs howled and demanded to be off. This was more like 'Hark to fifty Bountys'. Soon the huntsman gathered his pack and off they set across the fields around the village. I hoped the brown hares' long, black-tipped ears got fair warning of their coming and galloped away. The sight of a hunt with lovely dogs and horses, the red and black coats of the hunters and oh that lovely sound of the horn is exciting. What a shame it has to end with a killing. Would not a drag hunt be just as exciting? In this the dogs chase a trail of aniseed laid by the huntsman.

The huntsman prepares for the 'off'

A fine set of stocks on the smaller of Bolton-By-Bowland's greens

Since that time I have come to love the peace and tranquility of the village and the stroll across the fields to Sawley with the ruins of its Cistercian Abbey. Bolton by Bowland has two village greens, the smaller of which, opposite the Coach and Horses Inn, has a finely preserved set of stocks. To reach the second green follow the road to Gisburn but be sure to pause to look at the magnificent church of St. Peter and St. Paul on the left. The church mainly dates from the 13th century although there was at least one building on the site prior to this date. It is the tower, although it was rebuilt in 1852, which provides students of architecture with most food for thought because it is so different from the normal design seen in these parts. The answer may well lie with King Henry VIth, who spent some time in hiding at Bolton Hall with his loyal servant Sir Ralph Pudsay. Henry's army had been routed at Hexham in 1464 and the King was obliged to flee. At this time Sir Ralph was rebuilding the church and it is thought that the monarch influenced the design of the tower which shows similarities to those in Somerset with which Henry was certainly familiar. The unfortunate monarch was later captured whilst crossing the river Ribble near Clitheroe and was taken to London where he died. In the grounds of Bolton Hall there is also King Henry's well which he is said to have designed and used as a swimming pool. Alas the once fine hall was demolished earlier this century but the gateposts can still be seen opposite the church and on either side of the private road leading down to the river are the remnants of the once famous gardens. Sir Ralph has a more permanent record of his efforts on display in the church for here is a memorial slab to the fertile knight, his three wives and twenty five children!

The Church of St. Peter and St. Paul, the design of which shows the influence of the unfortunate Henry VIth

The village itself dominated the area for centuries and in the reign of Edward III (1327-1377) a market charter was granted, and much of eastern Bowland was governed from here. Beyond the church is the second, and by far the largest, of the two greens. The side nearest the road is fringed with trees whilst the centre section of the row of buildings opposite is the old courthouse on the roof of which is a weather vane in the shape of a fox. Although this green looks the most impressive it is doubtless the smaller one which is the oldest since here are the stocks and the stump of what was probably the old market cross. In the Domesday book the village was listed as Bodeton and later as Bolton-juxta-Bowland which is a very accurate description for a settlement on the edge of Bowland Forest which is also on the fringe of Ribblesdale. A series of lovely walks from the village lead into both these attractive areas. It is almost possible to follow the route taken by the eccentric William Pudsay who, fleeing from the authority of Elizabeth 1st, is reputed to have jumped his horse off a high cliff and over the river Ribble and made good his escape. The tale which is told to explain what has become known as Pudsay's Leap is obviously an intricate weave of a weft of fact but with a more substantial warp of fiction! Whilst on the brink of bankruptcy, William was riding in the forest when he met a group of 'little people' who gave him a magic bit for his horse and also told the whereabouts of a rich vein of silver. William quickly restored his fortunes by minting his own coins but Queen Elizabeth on hearing about this was far from amused. The story continues by relating William's escape and his horse protected by the magic bit jumped the impossible gorge across the Ribble and made his way to London. He did have some influence with the Queen, who was his godmother, but although he kept his head on his shoulders his mines, which were probably in the Rimington area, were confiscated. Not all the tale is ficticious however, because several of the Pudsay shillings marked with an escallop and which William minted are still to be seen in collections.

Whenever I visit Bolton-by-Bowland I think of that first occasion when the rain swept down and the hunt gathered, but whilst writing this chapter I was more fortunate. The autumn day had been hot and the hedgerows were ablaze with colour from rowan, hawthorn and rose fruits. I had collected a couple of pounds of sloes from the blackthorn trees and was thinking of brewing my sloe gin which would keep me warm on many a winter's walk. It was dark when I reached my car and I had not realised that the real excitment of the day was yet to come. I had just passed the cosy old pub, the Copy Nook, when I had to brake hard as a sika deer stag stood defiantly in the centre of the road, no doubt dazzled by the headlights. Bowland has always been famous for its deer and it was smashing to see such a splendid stag but I could not help hoping that the native red deer will sometime return to its old haunts. The Japanese Sika was introduced into Britain in the 19th century as a park animal and the present Bowland animals are probably the remnants of a herd kept by Lord Ribblesdale at Gisburne Park. If I can't have the red then the delightfully alert sikas can be sure of a welcome in my list of the wildlife of Bowland.

Chapter Ten
Bridges over the Hodder

Bowland's largest river, the Hodder, widens and deepens until it joins the Ribble close to the pleasant village of Hurst Green between Whalley and Longridge. A delightful and well signed walk begins at Higher Hodder Bridge below the Inn of the same name and twists along an undulating route to Lower Hodder Bridge and the river's confluence with the Ribble. Most of the path passes through tangled trees and drifts of flowers and Hodder Woods have been known and loved by naturalists for many years. It is not just local folk who know the woods because of the works of the poet Gerard Manley Hopkins (1844-1889). This shy man was a Jesuit teacher at the nearby Stonyhurst College who found perhaps the only real peace in his life during his wanderings through Hodder Woods. The surrounding hills were also well known to the poet who wrote about the kestrel thus:

The Windhover

To Christ our Lord

I caught this morning morning's minion, kingdom of
daylight's dauphin, dapple-dawn-dawn Falcon, in his riding
Of the rolling level underneath his steady air, and striding
high there, how he rung upon the rein of a wimpling wing
In his ecstasy! then off, off forth on swing.
As a skate's heel sweeps smooth on a bow-bend: the hurl
and gliding
Rebuffed the big wind. My heart in hiding
Stirred for a bird, the achieve of, the mastery of the thing!
Brute beauty and valour and act, oh, air, pride, plume, here
Buckle! AND the fire that breaks from the thee then, a billion
Times told lovelier, more dangerous, O my chevalier!

No wonder of it: sheer plod makes plough down sillion
Shine, and blue-bleak embers, ah my dear,
Fall, gall themselves, and gash gold-vermillion.

Whilst I find some of the language used by Hopkins a little difficult I know of no other poet who captures the atmosphere of the Hodder valley so well.

My own fondest memory of Hodder woods takes me back to early dawn on a beautifully gentle spring morning whilst I was preparing to record a radio programme of the dawn chorus. Blackbird, song thrush, robin, wren and willow warbler were all soon in full song and as the pink flush of dawn crept through the trees a sleepy sounding tawny owl joined in sounding, I thought, a little sad that the hunting night was over. Above the surrounding fields a curlew's bubbling call blended with the soaring notes of the skylark. Soon the morning light revealed the full glory of a bluebell wood filled with an azure mist and heavy scent. Dotted among the sea of blue were the white star like heads of ramsons which looked like jewels and smelled like garlic!

Kingfishers, dippers and grey wagtails are resident along this stretch of river and I am always sorry when I reach Lower Hodder bridge and meet up with the modern world speeding along the Longridge to Whalley road. For a lover of bridges, however there is some consolation for here are two spans. Standing on one bridge it is possible to look downstream at a splendidly proportioned packhorse bridge built in 1562 by Richard Shireburn at a cost of £70. Locals refer to this as Cromwell's Bridge in the belief that the Protector stayed at the Shireburn's mansion at Stonyhurst in August 1648 and marched his army over the bridge. It is, however, a narrow bridge for a large army and its cumbersome ordnance and luggage and it is much more likely that the Hodder was forded at a point close to the meeting with the Ribble at Wincley.

To discover what happened to the Shireburn family and their mansion of Stonyhurst we must take a look at the village of Hurst Green turning right at the Shireburn Arms. To the right is a row of Alms Houses looking as if they

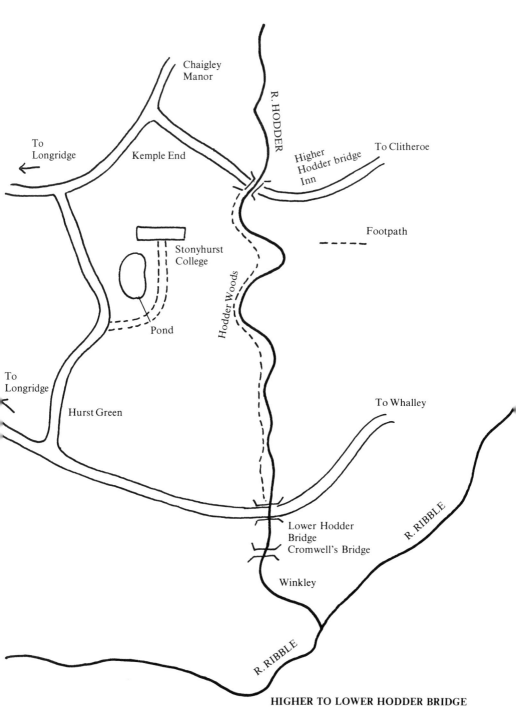

HIGHER TO LOWER HODDER BRIDGE

had been there for centuries. If you read the inscription you see that they were built in 1706 at Kemple End some $3\frac{1}{2}$ miles away and close to the Higher Hodder bridge! In 1946 they were carefully removed and reassembled for the use of workers employed by the school. Few stately homes in the North of England have fared so well as Stonyhurst despite it having such an unlucky start. Whilst Sir Nicholas Shireburn was watching his new house being built his young and only son died after having eaten yew berries. Nicholas died in 1717 and his daughter who was married to the Duke of Norfolk, a prominent Catholic supporter, inherited the estate. After the death of the Duchess of Norfolk, Stonyhurst came into the hands of Thomas Weld who, in 1794, leased the house to a teaching order - the Jesuits. Thomas Weld's son, also called Thomas became a Cardinal and the future of the school was thus assured and has thrived ever since. Stonyhurst has a long tradition of academic excellence and famous old scholars include the actor Charles Laughton and Sir Arthur Conan Doyle. Some experts have suggested that the 'Hounds of the Baskervilles' may have been based on the mists which sometimes clothe the hills of East Lancashire, but he must also have known its more gentle side.

I have often sat among the bilberries and heather around Kemple End listening to the June cuckoo, the male calling without apparent pause for breath, whilst his silent mate seeks out the nest of a meadow pipit in which to slyly slip her egg for the host to incubate and then struggle to feed the comparatively huge infant. I also remember the same spot on breezy April mornings when the first wheatears of the year flit among the stone walls and their white rumps flash in the sunlight. Kemple End has the rugged grandeur typical of Northern moorlands and yet its wilderness is tempered by the presence of cosy hotels and villages with smoke rising in spires from the chimneys of the cottages.

This is something of a contrast to the windswept heights of the Trough of Bowland which blocks the opposite end of the Hodder valley.

Chapter Eleven
Dunsop Bridge and the Trough of Bowland

Old Stables near Thorneyholme, Dunsop Bridge

I sat quietly eating a cream tea in the lounge of the Thorneyholme Hotel looking out into the gardens and watching the raindrops reflecting the rays of the afternoon sun. After the shower came the heat and the stream of water vapour evaporating from the well-tended lawns carried the scent of newly cut grass.

From Dunsop Bridge Car Park there are three possible walks. Two follow the course of the River Hodder. The path downstream leads to Whitewell, whilst an equally pleasant route upstream leads to Newton.

The third crosses a bridge over the river, through the village of Dunsop Bridge and then up to the famous Trough of Bowland with its splendidly savage scenery. I can never resist a short stroll downstream to the point where the River Dunsop merges with the Hodder. There is no finer river scenery than this. A common sandpiper called to its young which were hiding under the umbrella-like leaves of a butterbur, and trout were leaping out of the deep pools to catch the insects on the clear surface of the water.

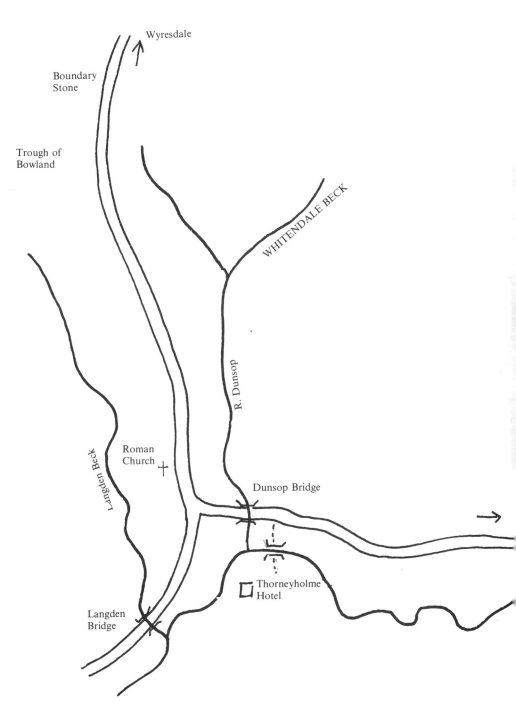

Wyresdale

Boundary
Stone

Trough of
Bowland

WHITENDALE BECK

R. Dunsop

Langden Beck

Roman
Church

Dunsop Bridge

Thorneyholme
Hotel

Langden
Bridge

*The Boundary Stone, until 1974 the County Boundary between Lancashire and Yorkshire,
still guards the entrance to the Trough of Bowland.*

Kingfisher

The Towneley family of Burnley had strong connections with Dunsop Bridge, and the old stables at Thorneyholme housed many of the family's horses and their fine cattle have grazed the fields around these parts for centuries. The most famous of all the animals was the racehorse Kettledrum which won the 1861 Derby at the long odds of 16-1.

All the locals seem to have benefited and it is said that St. Hubert's church, sited on the left of the road from Dunsop Bridge into the Trough of Bowland, was financed by the winnings. The church, consecrated in 1865, is Roman Catholic as we would expect if connected with the Towneleys. Kettledrum was trained at Stud Farm and the dark chestnut stallion with three white stockings was famous for miles around.

The whole of Dunsop appears to have been one huge stud farm and although one fascinating set of stables on the site of the present trout hatchery has long been demolished, others of equally impressive dimensions remain. Apparently, there was even a horse bath in one of the boxes long before the majority of houses had such luxury! There were also small holes in the doors so that grooms could inspect their valuable charges without disturbing them.

The local roads must always have been busy with important traffic and at the junction of the road into Dunsop Bridge is the original finger signpost dated 1739 which tells us that Clitheroe is seven miles, Lancaster 11 miles and Hornby 10 miles, whilst the distance to Slaidburn has been eroded by the weather. The modern signpost over it disputes the distances and the spelling by listing Slaidburn as four miles, Clitheroe at 11 and reflecting the decline in the influence of Hornby by not mentioning it at all.

Lancaster via the Trough of Bowland is given as 14½ miles and it was the road that I chose to drive slowly up to the boundary stone at the head of the pass. This marks the junction of the old counties of Lancashire and Yorkshire before the boundaries were altered in 1974.

After parking near the Summit and eating my supper at the boundary stone, I enjoyed the steep descent alongside the Langden Beck which, like the Dunsop, joins the Hodder but not before giving up most of its catchment to the water board.

Despite the loss of many trees from Tudor times onwards a considerable amount of planting took place in the early 19th century when Fenton-Cawthorne purchased 1,500 acres of land on both sides of the Trough summit. On the Yorkshire side a great deal of lime burning took place, but shelterbeds of pines and other conifers were planted for game and sheep.

From his vantage point at Wyresdale Tower, Fenton looked down into Lancashire. From the boundary stone the route of the small tributaries to the Hodder can be seen on the Bowland side. A look to the west reveals a panoramic view of the river Wyre. But this is another route to be saved and savoured for another day. Wyresdale has a charm all of its own!